CW00500121

Listening
in the
Silence

Poems and Reflections
When God Seems Distant

Hilary Allen

Copyright © Hilary Allen 2022

All rights reserved. No part of this publication may be reproduced, stored in a retrieval system, or transmitted in any form by any means, electronic, mechanical, photocopying or otherwise, without the prior written consent of the publisher. Short extracts may be used for review purposes.

ISBN: 978-1-907929-64-9

You can contact Hilary Allen at:
seeinginthedark824@gmail.com

www.lifepublications.org.uk

Commendations

This anthology provides delightful, contemporary reflections on familiar scriptures, helping the reader to experience the sacred text from the deepest recesses of the soul. Read, ruminate and enjoy!

Paul Bown, Christian Worker

These poems and reflections are a treasure store to be read silently or out loud. I found myself deeply moved more than once, as Hilary paints a picture through her words, of God's love and grace for all of us, wherever we might be on our journey through life.

Mel Moore, fellow Street Pastor

Listening in the Silence is the natural sequel to Hilary's first book, *Seeing in the Dark*. Listening in the silence when God seems distant, encourages us to be still and to wait for God's words to come through the deafening silence when, in times of trouble, He appears to be absent. Hilary's words, reminding us of God's unending love, offer comfort and peace to all who will listen.

Christine Davies, Christian wildlife advocate

I read *Listening in the Silence* with my heart open. The words transported me to a place of joy, pain and new decisions. Not simply printed words, but beautiful and at times challenging. The pieces spoke aloud to me. I listened and welcomed their voices into my inner self.

Hyanghee, a follower of Jesus

Listening in the Silence touched my heart and soul. I'm definitely not a poet and reading poetry is not something I would normally do, but I have felt compelled to say how much this book has helped me through some difficult times. The first poem in the book, *Listening in the Silence* has words that are so poignant, and in my quiet, silent times helped me so much. Another piece *God Hasn't Finished,* is a real reminder for me that God hasn't finished what He started, and will we allow Him to continue? I certainly will! Thank you Hilary.

Glyn Legg, Retired Engineer

Hilary's second book *Listening in the Silence*, is welcomed as we strive to grasp a closer relationship with God, to make sense of our existence in a challenging world. She writes with empathic understanding, guiding one towards the sustained comfort and love spoken from God. Hilary's poems include Bible characters in both Old and New Testaments who in troubled times sought help from God. She reminds us that God is here for us all, when we open our ears and hearts to Him, to receive inner peace in moments of prayerful silence.

Sue Casson, wife, mum and grandma

Silence can often be very scary, particularly when our relationship with God is involved. Using the power of the gift of expression which God has given her, Hilary has

4

shown that these spaces need not be scary, but rather enlightening, comforting and even faith-assuring. She delights to encourage us not only to enter into the innermost thoughts of some biblical characters, but also where we can ourselves engage with God along and in life's often fragile and broken circumstances. Be blessed and encouraged as you *"Listen in the Silence"*.

Jan Adams, mum and grandma

Listening in the Silence is a treasury of wonder and joy with so many spiritual insights. Sit down and quietly read of God and His amazing love in these thought-provoking pieces. Be blessed and encouraged through the prayers and promises as God shares His heart.

John Elford, Retired

Hilary's words come from experience. Sometimes they relate to specific times and places – the big times – but they also speak from the ordinary that can be found in everyday life.

We are invited to see things anew, to reflect, re-align, and above all to, listen, not just to hear, but listen with our whole being. In the great and small things of life Hilary invites us, "to linger in love, to respond and be satisfied", poems which speak of the extra ordinary in the ordinary and the common place in our experience of life.

William Newey, Chaplain, SomersetFT

Hilary writes from the heart, taking her inspiration from God's Word. Her work is a wonderful companion for prayerful devotions or to read alongside scripture. You really feel a sense of God speaking through her work, in those reflective and precious moments of silence that we so desperately need in our world today.

It is both an encouragement and affirmation of God's promises, helping each one of us to draw closer to God in our relationship with Him.

Lieutenant Heather Culshaw, Salvation Army

The Christian world has always had a rich blessing of seers and poets who see the world in different colours and bring it alive for the rest of us. Hilary Allen is such a person, who takes the Biblical and the ordinary and brings them to us so that we can actually picture the things spoken of in her poems.

Her poetry is visual, full of life and God's majesty weaves it way through each letter, word and phrase. I challenge anyone to not be inspired by the world that Hilary brings to life on the pages of this book. Very refreshing…

Rev Mark Brown, Minister of Granshaw Presbyterian Family Church, N Ireland

From the Author

In these challenging times I find myself listening so much to those I come alongside. Hearing of the many diverse struggles and personal issues, as they are shared.

Writing poetry, exploring with the backdrop of Biblical characters and God's word, I have sought to understand and express that God is not distant from us and our troubles.

I treasure how God's never-ending love reaches us wherever we are. God is present and we can hear Him.

Hilary

Index

Listening in the Silence

There is a silence beyond words
where speechless prayer is uttered
within the silence of the soul
God may whisper
into our listening.

Listening

Invited
to listen
to draw breath
to quench thirst
to hear God's heart
to linger in love
to respond
and be satisfied
with God.

Psalm 63:1-5

Frost

There is a corner of the garden
where winter sun has not stretched.
Where frost unyielding
imprisons the stark neglected scrub
and reckless bitter wind
whips its vice-like hold.
Welcome Love's warm breath.
Grace will become visible
through flourishing,
thriving abundantly.
God yet restores.

Joel 2:25

Snowdrops

Fragile, bowed, enduring.
Light in the darkest of nights.
Sentinels of hope
as earth's beauty is re-born
and barrenness transformed.
Watch God's certain promise
of new tomorrows.

Psalm 92:4

Light

And God said,
  "Let there be light."
And the Light stirred creation into life:
And bacteria breed, ants forage
moths flutter, butterflies bask
dragonflies dance, chameleons camouflage
bees pollinate, lilies glorify
the thrush chorales at dawn
herons fish, stars twinkle
the moon reflects
the rainbow promises
harvest flourishes.

And God sent
  One to be the Light.
And Jesus entered our world
living, showing, loving, touching, teaching,
healing, transforming, liberating, promising,
dying, forgiving, redeeming, saving.

And God gives
  His light to us
keeping, guarding, interceding, companioning,

14

guiding, teaching, leading, enlightening, strengthening, nurturing, healing, Christ-like making.

And God asks
  what do *you* do with His Light?

Genesis 1:3-4
John 8:12
John 16:13

Hagar

God is a God who sees
all my distress.
God is a God who comforts
when all alone.
God is a strong arm
on which to rely.
God is a God who knows
for He counts my tears.
God is a God who feels
so tenderly will carry.
God is a God who doesn't give up.
He picks the pieces
of my brokenness
gently shaping them,
refining them,
until they radiate
His glory.

Genesis 16:1-15

Sarah

Waiting is so very tough.
When is waiting long enough?
Months stretch into empty years
deepening anguish and bitter tears.
Silently, hope drifts to despair
no solace, comfort anywhere.
Heartache wrings my soul of peace
when will the waiting ever cease?
Yet God in His unbounded time
chooses purposes divine.
Only He knows when time is right;
in my old age He shows His might.
Relying on God's voice I yield,
yet cannot say how God will heal.
God crafts His wonders His own way
and in our lives His grace displays.

Genesis 18:1-15, 21:1-7

Jacob

Stop!

You're never satisfied!
Stop your grasping,
you're ever wanting;
you keep resisting
what God could be doing
in you.
God hates your cheating
and your pretending;
cease fighting
your cause,
have done with scheming.
Stop running
give up hiding.
God is always seeing,
purposing
for your blessing;
Jacob, God wants you fathering
a nation honouring
the one true God.
Changing
and naming
you Israel, meaning
one who is triumphing
with God.

Genesis 28:10-22

Joseph

Forgiveness

There is repentance in forgiveness;
confession of how I fail.
There is choice in forgiveness,
a deliberate letting go.
There is freedom in forgiveness,
released from others' wrongs.
There is healing through forgiveness,
no longer can it hurt.
There is a process of forgiveness,
continuing day by day.
There is wholeness through forgiveness,
bringing health and peace.
There is grace in forgiveness,
with relationships restored.
There is prayer throughout forgiveness,
as the loving Helper comes.
There is strength in forgiveness,
to determine to do good.
There's all-sufficient forgiveness
in God who came to save.
There is hope in forgiveness
to flourish and know joy.

Genesis 50:15-21

Moses and the Burning Bush

Unusual, unexpected,
unexplained unconsumed
bush.
Uneasy, unshod, unworthy,
unsettled, uncertain, unprepared,
unfit, unsure, unthinkable,
unable, unfolding understanding.
"Moses,
I AM with you always."
Encounter with God.
Enabled, empowered, encouraged,
envisioned, emboldened,
endorsed, engaged.
Envoy of God

Exodus 3:1-14

My People

You are My people
I will never abandon you.
When you are overwhelmed
when there is no way out
when all is lost,
I AM.
There is no need to fear
no reason to despair nor give up.
Stop running.
Be still.
Let go your feeble plans.
Stand firm.
Be confident in all I do,
watch how I will act for you.
You are My precious people
which nothing on earth can ever change.
I AM working for you
I AM your hope
I AM your God.

Exodus 14:8-22

Hannah

God,
why don't You act, change things?
What do I do with my pain?
I am ashamed, I'm insulted, ridiculed.
I live with the anguish of the empty years,
the agony of hopelessness.
It hurts so very much:
It breaks me inside.
God, I want to hear You in this silence!

Prayer lifts me to God.
I look away from myself
to Him, the God of all the universe.

God does hear me!
Almighty God does hear!
Almighty God does know!
He knows my every cry,
He sees each one of my tears
in His silence.
And in His silence,
unseen
He tenderly holds me close.
Tells me to trust in the waiting
in the grim uncertainty.

And in that barren waiting
in Your silence
I give to You what I desire most
I stop holding on to what I want
I let go and cling to You.
For God, You work
deep within.
I realise You are able
to take my cares and treasure them with
utmost diligence.
Growing within me is a wonder
at the completeness of Your love.
A love which takes me as I am:
A love that is not dependent on my ability
to respond.
I leave all with You.
You met me in the silence.
You have heard me.
God You know
 and when the time is right, You act.

1 Samuel 1-2:10

Samuel

A call in the darkness
a consecration
a willingness
a resolution
to obey God
just where he was
faithful and open
day after day
step by step
a co-operation with God
as fully as he knew
until God led further
to follow His way
to trust His will
just where he was.
Such is true greatness.

1 Samuel 3:1-19

Elijah

Nowhere

There's nowhere to run in this darkness
no place to hide away
nothing left to give You
no heart even to pray.
No one to come and befriend me
nobody of faith to stand;
no knowing how You will act
or declare Your reign in the land.

There's no place where God is absent,
nothing beyond His care,
providing food and refreshing,
Your power You now declare:
Not present in shattering rock
nor in the shaken earth.
Not in the fire's purity
but in whispers of precious worth:

"What are you doing here Elijah?
Go back the way you came.
As you journey, I will guide you;
in obeying, My name you proclaim."

1 Kings 19:1-18

Lord, It's Hard

Lord, it's hard to hear You in the storm,
struggling alone, feeling lost and forlorn,
adrift in my pain, knowing doubts and fears,
sunk in despair with my sorrows and tears,
or when I'm drained and feeling the stress,
wearied by long nights of sleeplessness.

Lord, it's hard to hear You in the calm;
insuring my peace, so buffered from harm,
enjoying life's goodness and days of ease,
the richness of friendships and families,
cushioned from need by adequate wealth,
fulfilling my dreams, keeping good health.

Lord, it's hard to hear You
when I'm not listening.

Psalm 13

Wait for the Lord

Waiting is searching for purpose
 reaching out in uncertainty
 silencing distractions
 longing for light
 enduring in trust
 listening expectantly
 facing truth
 resting in God
 submitting, yielding
 receiving mercy
 discovering wisdom
 transforming, re-creating
 strengthening faith
 knowing peace
 enlarging vision
 enriching hope
Waiting is abiding in God.

Psalm 27:14

In the Stillness

When you are still
when you are listening
then you can receive the truth
that I AM God.
Did you forget?
Or doubt I could or would?
Be still.
Let Me share My heart
let Me comfort your soul
let Me pour My peace into
the parched places of your life.
Be still and know for yourself
that I am God.
In all things
I work
My purpose
for your good.

Psalm 46:10

Seek God

In the pain which drowns all other sense
seek God alone.
In the heartache of desolation
with searing loss
and numbing indecision
seek God alone.
In fear which sweeps away true hope
or brokenness which doesn't mend
seek God alone.
In anger's fire
in that most cruel injustice
seek God alone.
Amidst the terrors
He surprises
blessing with Himself
never withholding;
secure in God's hands
for He never lets us go.

Psalm 62:5-8

The Little Wave

"Save me! I'm drowning!" the wee wave
wails,
anguished, assaulted, adrift and assailed.
Singing, then stinging, spat from the surge,
rising then crashing, chaotic, submerged.
Ceaseless crescendo, then smashed in the surf,
hidden and hollow, howling the hurt.
"Drifting! I'm drifting!" down, down to the
deep,
drawn and discovering the source that keeps
absorbing my terror and treasures my worth,
bathes me with balm, sweetly sating my thirst.
Then I'm moving, I'm growing, I'm rising
again.
Empowered, ennobled, I'm sparkling again!

Psalm 69:1-5, 13-18

Hiding Place

You are my hiding place
found by deep unchanging grace
poured into my heart so freely
overflowing me.
Come, reach out
draw me,
open, unresisting,
close
to Yourself.

Psalm 91

Joy

Joy is God's good gift
   receive it.
Joy is God's faithful love
   believe it.
Joy is God's wise voice
   hear it.
Joy is God with us
   realise it.
Joy is a thankful heart
   cultivate it.
Joy is an obedient will
   flourish with it.
Joy is a trusting soul
   rest in it.
Joy is for giving away
   share it.
Joy is in forgiving
   do it.
Joy is a way of life
   live it.

Psalm 100

The Beach

Deserted dunes,
debris, driftwood.
Broken shells,
garish plastic shards
sprinkled with sea-salt.
Fag ends entwined
by sinuous seaweed.
Limp football, abandoned spade.
Washed-up crabs squatting
in wrecked sandcastles:
Beyond the littered beach
an azure sea stretches to touch the powdered
sky;
rocks and sand sculpture the land
defining perspective and purpose.
Asserting that I too
can unload my burdens here
and like the deep
know the call and turning
of Your tide.

Psalm 103:3-12

According to Your Word

A prayer

God,
unveil Yourself within Your word
that I may discern Your ways.
Illumine thought and deed
that I may follow after You.
Convict my soul to know forgiveness
that I may find true liberation.
Infuse Your promises with strength to trust
that I may anchor fast my love.
Satisfy my deep longing
through the all-sufficiency of Your grace.

Amen.

Psalm 119:97-105

$\mathcal{P}$salm 121

Who will help me?
Where will my help come from?
I recount the yesterdays
which proved with certainty
that God, You were there.
You led through the darkness
met my doubt with mercy
fed my soul
sheltered me safe in the storms
gave courage in my fear.
In faith, I reach out today
trusting there will be
a tomorrow of purpose,
knowing You never leave me.

Psalm 121

All This Time

All this time,
I have been longing to know you.
Expectant, even before I gave you breath.
Delighting in the design of your dainty form.
Patiently parenting as you grew.
Whispering My love
through care and creation and joy.
Transfixed, unable to take My eyes off you,
I called through your busyness.
Holding out My hand in your hurt.
Wounded, when you reasoned Me away.
Watching your distractions, your search for
peace,
Waiting, knowing that what you needed most is
Me.
Child, time is short.
Your days are full.
Know that all I want
is to be with you.
Always.

Psalm 139:13-18, 23-24

This Day

Lord,
this day You invite me to know You,
    to keep company with You.
This day I will seek to honour You,
    to live in dependence on You.
This day I will seek to be faithful to Your truths,
    to discern Your wisdom.
This day I will seek to enjoy Your blessings,
    to be thankful for Your mercy.
This day I will seek to obey Your heart,
    to love without condition.
This day I will seek to discover Your direction,
    to trust in Your goodness.
This day I will seek to let go of hurt,
    to strive to live in peace.
This day I will seek to endure,
    to reach out for Your strength.
This day I desire
    to know You.

Proverbs 3:3-6

The Clay

The clay does not say to the potter:
What are you doing?
How long will it take?
What will I be?
How am I going to be treated?
Why have you made me like this?
Why the breaking apart?
Why a re-making?
Where will I be used?
I didn't expect fire,
I didn't expect to be put aside,
I don't want this!
Until I see
that Your image
is being fashioned in me.

Isaiah 45:9, Romans 9:21

Promises

Promises, promises, promises
from God who is faithful, almighty and wise.
God who always works good in our lives.
Promises for the seed-time, the harvest and rain,
sustaining, providing in plenty and in pain.
The promise of a new life with Jesus to share,
forgiveness, salvation, His comfort, His care.
The promise of peace in the storms that we face,
His guidance, revelation, His power and His grace.
The promise He hears us whenever we pray,
attentively nurtures, day after day.
The promise of God's Spirit who comes alongside,
unceasing, Christ-like making, 'til to glory we rise.
His promise to watch o'er each step we take,
to lead us, to teach us and never forsake.
Promises to discover, to believe God keeps,
promises leading us God-ward to seek.
Promises which prove God to be
trustworthy, loving to you and to me.

Lamentations 3:22-26

Who Would Have Thought It?

God comes
as a baby.
Immortality
wrapped in cloth
laid on straw
vulnerable
weak
crying for milk.
Who would have thought it?
Only God.

John 1:14

Dancing

Have you seen
the dancing in the skies?
Have you heard
exuberant angels' praise?
Have you felt
the wonderment of God becoming man?
Have you found
His love that brought us near?
Have you known
God's eternal peace?
Have you danced?

Luke 2:13-15

Meeting the Christ-child

"**W**hat's in your hands?" the babe enquired,
"more frankincense, or myrrh or gold?"

"I didn't know what to bring you,
what you'd like, I wasn't told.
There's nothing much of real worth
that I've bundled into my sack;
it's a tangled mess of sadness
and weighs heavy upon my back.
There's hurt and unforgivingness
which I've carried for far too long;
the love I never gave away
and regret from the years long gone;
there's anger in the words I spat
and the bitter tears I have wept:
My selfishness which failed to help
and the thanklessness I kept.
But gifts are there of my service,
of time and of blessings shared;
promises held when life was tough
and prayers for the ones I cared."

"Child, please let go your sin and shame
all your load I'll take and claim.
Complete forgiveness in My love
is yours to own, that's why I came."

John 3:16-17

The Wise Men

Will you come?

Will you come and worship?
Will you seek His star?
Will you choose to give Him
all you have and are?

Will you enter humbly?
Will you bend your knee?
Will you let Him change you?
From sin and pride He'll free!

Will you stay and linger
not rush on your way?
Will you hold His presence
to light your path today?

Matthew 2:1-12

Anna

Lord, why can't I be like Anna,
delighting myself in You?
I see in the script of her story
the sadness and pain she worked through.
She was widowed, lost her future;
wept bitter tears of despair.
Yet her grief was transformed to gladness
for her life wasn't finished there.
With You she faced the bleak present,
Your comfort and solace knew.
Her struggle became a surrender;
in trust, a true joy and peace grew.
Ignored by many, You chose her
to recognise and reveal God's will;
in waiting she learnt to flourish;
saw the promise of Messiah fulfilled.

Luke 2:36-38

The Sower Speaks

What kind of heart will receive My love?
Not one that's indifferent or cold.
What kind of heart will grow My love?
Not one that gives up in the storms.
What kind of heart will nurture My love?
Not one that goes after the world.
What kind of heart will share My love?
The one that is enriched by Me.
What kind of heart have you?

Matthew 13:1-9

The Treasure Seeker

There is a searching and a seeking;
unearthing and discovering.
There is joy in the finding;
delight in the realising.
There is blessing in belonging;
preciousness of possessing.
There is treasure of utmost worth.
There is a price to be paid
an ultimate cost to be given
which demands everything.

Matthew 13:46

Simon Peter

I went to find you, Jesus.
You asked me to follow You.
I invited You into my home.
You transformed everything
in the healing of my mother-in law.
You commandeered my boat, my livelihood.
I grasped the wisdom, the truth You taught.
That day, You told us to fish once more,
after a night of useless work.
In the full sun of midday! Ridiculous!
We did do as You asked.
We did put out into the deep,
despite our utter weariness and disbelief.
We had nothing left to give.
Then the miracle happened.
All those fish! (And more hard work!)
More nets breaking! (And mending all over
again!)
My boat beginning to sink!
Slowly I realised that obeying You
would cost me everything.

Yet a greater miracle happened inside me.
You showed me, the savvy fisherman,
that nothing and no one is beyond
Your reach and power.

Jesus, you exposed the real me!
The failure that I am;
blundering, inadequate, blind, self-seeking.
"Go away!" I pleaded.
But you didn't.
You loved me enough to work a deeper miracle.
You changed me!

Luke 5:1-11

Disciples in the Boat

First a chill as the wind whipped up;
the sky darkening, evening racing in.
The storm threatening.
I'm angry we had left it so late:
I would have organised this better.
It's foolish to set sail at this hour.
What was He thinking of?
I should have trusted in my own judgement;
relied on all my experience.
This storm is grim.
I'm not sure I can handle this.
Jesus has gone to sleep! Opted out. Left us to
it.
Forgotten us. Doesn't bother.
The raging sea makes me grit my teeth, steel
myself.
Soaked, salt stinging sharp in my eyes.
Lunging, then rising in churning waves.
Battered. Frightened. Terrified. Exhausted.
Sinking. Losing everything.
"Why did You let this happen?
Don't You care?"
Jesus woke. Commands wind and sea.
Speaks "Peace. Be still."

What was He doing coming into my boat?
Coming into my familiar, ordinary world?
Changing not just the sea, the wind,
but me!

Luke 8:22-25

If Only

If only there was another way
if only I knew Jesus could
if only He knew what it took
if only a touch
if only I was completely healed
If only I could hide my shame
if only I could melt away
if only He hadn't noticed me,
called me out.
Only so He could heal,
restore, forgive, renew
and make me whole.

Luke 8:43-48

Is There Enough?

Always last
always at the back
left behind
missing out.
Watching loaded baskets empty,
hungry hands grasping.
Will there be enough
for me?
There is plenty,
overflowing abundance,
more than enough to satisfy
of food
of His words
of life.

Luke 9:10-17

The Gardener's Plea

Leaves aren't enough
I'm looking for fruit,
fruit that's mature and ripe.
With My cultivation
you will flourish,
My nurture and care will suffice.
Leaves aren't enough
to grow who you are;
receive, be fed by Me.
Let My goodness nourish your roots;
develop fruit by abiding with Me.

Luke 13:6-9

Father Waits

I wait
I watch expectantly
I will never give you up
I'm always thinking of you.
I will wait
for you to come,
for you to know the longing in My heart,
My love without limits.
I will wait
relishing the delight of embracing you,
of having you home
with Me.

Luke 15:11- 32

Two Brothers

The older brother said,
I always worked hard
I put in hours over and above
I was dutiful, doing all I was asked
I saved and never wasted a penny.
Surely my father is proud of me?

The other brother
squandered the family fortune
lived to please himself
risked life on the edge
then destitute, returned home.
Yet he knew father loved him
as he came back
into relationship with him.

Luke 15:11-32

The Healed Leper

There is
strength from the scars
beauty from the brokenness
a transforming of tragedy
re-shaping of the ugliness
an abundance from the barrenness.
Discovering God is not hidden.
Realizing His purpose
His triumph of love,
in me.

Luke 17:11-18

Persistent Prayer

So is it a test, a trial of faith,
or even temptation not to pray?
To give up when prayer's unanswered or fails?
Or is there more that God wants to say?

Does something happen when I can persist?
Is faith deepened, renewed, refined?
Does healing transform my sorrows and hurts?
Is waiting infused with Love Divine?

Does compassion move to serve and give?
Can I receive God's abundant grace?
Believing, I pray God will keep me held
until I'm drawn into His embrace.

Luke 18:1, 1 Thessalonians 5:17

Bartimaeus

Compassion Road

On the streets, existing and abused.
The blind misery of inner darkness
renders me useless.
My heart deserted and left begging
for a crust of someone's love.
Failure is an open wound
that never heals;
lacking courage strong enough to change.
Who will give me hope?

Jesus have mercy on me!
I want to see, Jesus!

Emerging
from my broken shell
into the bright light of living
I see Jesus!
He frees my prison of fear
liberates from guilt and shame
dissolves the anger
enables me to discover
all God will do in me!

Luke 18:35-43

Zacchaeus

I thought I was hidden in a sycamore tree;
the crowds wouldn't look, no one would see.
Jesus, You stopped, knew I'd agree
to You coming to my home along with me.
No longer could I hide wretched, sinful me,
yet You still sought my company.
You said Your forgiveness would set me free
from guilt and greed and grasping glee.
"I want to be new!" was my earnest plea.
My heart was changed; that I didn't foresee.
My repentance real, others now can see!

Luke 19:1-10

Walking

You don't have to walk in darkness;
My light has always shone.
You don't have to walk unguided
the way you've always done.

There is a choice in every step
of life, if you would seek;
the way of prayer; a different act
or turning of the cheek.

I came to give you freedom's grace
to find a better way.
I ask that you would follow Me;
in love, My words obey.

John 1:1-5, 10-14, 18

A Samaritan Woman

Jesus came near when others shunned me,
found me out, beneath my veneer.
He laid bare all I had hidden
understood each unvoiced fear.
He affirmed and honoured me
spoke to my doubt and utter shame;
in me fashioned God's own image;
re-created, no more the same!

John 4:6-26

Have You Not Known Me?

Have I been so long with you
yet you do not know Me?
Have I walked along with you
yet you do not want Me?
Have I whispered into your soul
yet you disregard Me?
Have I blessed with My love
yet you decline Me?
Have I not dwelt with you?

John 14:5-14

Judas

Jesus,
I'm disappointed in You.
You're not what I had hoped for.
You're not what I expected.
A Messiah who should have been,
who should have done more.
Empty broken promises
shattered dreams.

Jesus
poured fresh water
lovingly caressed
my calloused, dusty feet.
He cradled them
not wanting me to go
not wanting me to stumble
out into the darkness.
He never turned away.
Certain loving kindness
until the very end.

John 13:1-30

Simon of Cyrene

I didn't ask for this

Just a bystander in the Temple;
observing the passion of a rabbi
who spoke of God as Father.
Watching Your bloodied, battered body
stagger and fall.
Feeling the pierce of Roman gaze
forcing me from the crowd
to carry your cross.
God, I didn't ask for this!
You were spent.
Your eyes stung by dust, pleading
"Walk with Me. Do this for Me. Share My
pain."
The spitting, jeering of the crowd, the agony,
the scorching sun on bleeding back,
the sweat, the tears.
God, I did not ask for this.
But God, You chose this!
We came to that hell.
Wood torn from my shoulders
and nailed to Your flesh.
And from that terror
I glimpsed that You did this for all humanity.

And God, You asked for this!
Son of God, only I carried Your cross of
torture.
I did not ask for this.
Yet into my rage and bitterness,
touching Your scarred hands,
You poured love and forgiveness.
And You transformed
my pain, my heart, my life.
Yet still You ask me
"May I walk with you and strengthen you
as you did once for Me?'

Luke 23:26

Mary at the Tomb

I didn't recognise You
until You called my name.
Jesus, I have seen and known
Your transforming power.
Now You ask me
not to hold on to what has been,
not to recount what is lost.
Rather free
Your irrepressible love
to empower me
to go out and tell.

John 20:10-18

Emmaus Travellers

Can I walk with you
as you struggle on your way?
Can I talk with you
and understand your heart?
Can I show you
costly sacrificial love?
Can I share with you
My truth infused with joy?
Can I give you
My resurrection hope?
Can I be with you?

Luke 24:13-35

Thomas

In life's ordinariness You found me.
You befriended me, taught me, discipled me.
You showed to me the kingdom of God.
I did believe;
I boldly claimed I'd die for You.
Yet that day,
I saw You naked,
humiliated, shamed, despised,
stumbling to a certain death.
I ran away, left You alone.
I abandoned my shattered dreams.
It was over.
When others said You lived
how could I believe?
How could I ever trust You again?

You found me
in my unbelief.
You invited me to Your side
to touch Your precious wounds.
You let me kneel
and adore in wonderment.
You forgave me
gave to me life and hope
joy, destiny and powerful faith.
My Lord, My God!
Find me now each new day.

John 20:26-29

Philip

You call
leave this place
of life-changing blessings
and follow an empty desert road.
You lead
each untrodden step.
You guide
in undiscovered ways.
You enable
growing dependency,
with richer depths of grace
in the joy of obedience.

Acts 8:26-39

Ananias

Surely not!
Anything but this.
It's a dangerous task.
He's a difficult person.
It's absurd.
Surely there's someone better.
Surely someone braver.
Surely someone with more experience.
But God You require
obedience not questioning
trust not doubting
commitment not comfort
faithfulness not self-pleasing
and courage which does not limit
Your wondrous ways.

Acts 9:1-19

No Conditions

No conditions
solely My call to come.
No barriers
save yours to be let down.
No condemnation
in My full forgiveness.
No demands
except you receive.
No cares
that I will not carry
No wrong
which I cannot redeem.
No person
whom I do not love.
No sacrifice
too great
for you.

Romans 8:1-2

Letting Go

God invites
hand over the hurts
let go of loss
give up hope deferred
leave care-worn burdens.
Yield, one by one.
No longer have you any need of these;
they are His now.
Empty hands
can hold the future
of His plans.

2 Corinthians 5:17

God is Waiting

I am waiting to bless you,
to fill you with the riches of My grace;
immense, inexhaustible.
Treasure all that I give.
Open your parched soul,
embrace My forgiveness
discern My wisdom
prove My all-sufficiency
incomparable, unlimited.
I wait for you to receive,
then
I can.

Ephesians 2:7

God Hasn't Finished

Did you know I want to change you,
on the inside, in your heart?
Had you forgotten that we're travelling
or are we journeying apart?
Not your treadmill of self-transformation,
with your struggles and defeat;
but a constant revolution
where My grace makes you complete.
Did you know you hadn't made it,
had you stopped, thought you'd arrived?
Let go your self-sufficiency,
your efforts and your pride.
Do you know I'm re-creating,
precious, unique, anew?
Will you allow Me to continue
My special work in you?

Philippians 1:6

The Little Acts of Faith

When you say no to ready temptation,
When you resist answering back,
When you travel the distance in loving care,
When you sacrifice your time,
When you honour God's name,
When you let go the grudge,
When you rejoice,
When you stop boasting about yourself,
When you show another the way,
When you allow God into your heart,
When you act justly,
When you touch the unloved,
When you care for creation,
When you are grateful to God,
When you pause to wonder and praise,
When you do what God says,
When you decline praise,
When you create,
When you trust in God,
When you share another's load,
When you build bridges,
When you open your hands and give,
When you listen to God,
When you say sorry,

When you apply God's word,
When you do not moan,
When you walk the extra mile,
When you intercede,
When you do not lie,
When you receive the grace of God,
When you say thank you,
When you weep alongside another,
When you refuse to deny God,
When you sow seeds of hope,
When you see with God's eyes,
When you forgive.
These are the victories,
the big acts of faith
today.

Philippians 2:12-16a

What More?

Child,
What more can I do to love you?
I created you in My image
I grieved at your sin and self-pleasing
I gave My Son to save you
I forgave and rescued you
I breathed Words to teach you
I enabled My Spirit's power to fill you
I opened heaven to you in prayer
I committed Myself to work within you
I always watch over you
I constantly am with you.
I treasure you.

Child,
Will you discover how much I love you,
allow My truth to speak into your heart,
open yourself to My healing?
Will you receive My forgiveness and grace,
realise My hope in you,
delight in being blessed?
Will you value the gifts I've given you,
know My peace
and let Me carry you?

Child,
What more can you do to love Me?

1 John 3:1-3

Heaven

God, lift me up
to certain hope
to wonder Heaven's indescribable beauty
to grasp the intangible fullness of Your
presence
to feel the longing that You have for me
and to revel in Your perfect love.
To envision pain and sorrow ceasing
and wholly be transformed.
And, as You lift me up,
I fall down
in true worship.

Revelation 22:1-5

Also by Hilary

Seeing in the Dark

A book of poems and reflections for when life gets tough.

To order a copy please contact:

seeinginthedark824@gmail.com